AF448516

Wheat Stalk

Swaying, not Severed

A Book Of Quotes On How To Tackle OCD,
Avoid Relapse And Sustain Recovery

By

Fatima Yusuf

Illustrated by Fernweh

Become
Shakespeare
.com

First published in 2020 by

BecomeShakespeare.com

One Point Six Technologies Pvt. Ltd.
119-123, 1st floor, Building No. J2, Wadala East,
Wadala Truck Terminal, Mumbai, Maharashtra 400037, India
T: +91 8080226699

Copyright © 2020, Fatima Yusuf

Wordit Art Fund helps deserving authors publish their work by providing monetary support. To apply for funding, please visit us at www.BecomeShakespeare.com

All rights reserved. Any unauthorized reprint or use of this material is prohibited. No part of this book may be reproduced or transmitted in any form or by any means, electronic or mechanical, including photocopying, recording, or by any information storage and retrieval system without express written permission from the author/publisher.

Please do not participate in or encourage piracy of copyrighted materials in violation of the author's rights. Purchase only authorized editions.

©

ISBN - 978-93-88942-89-8

CONTENTS

FOREWORD

To the readers…

The author of this self-help book 'Wheat Stalk: Swaying, not Severed', Fatima Yusuf has battled with obsessive compulsive disorder since the age of 13. In the book, she has presented her personal challenges and difficulty overcoming the disorder and how she graciously kept swimming through life with perseverance and faith.

Obsessive-Compulsive Disorder (OCD) is a common, chronic and long-lasting disorder in which a person has uncontrollable, reoccurring thoughts (obsessions) and behaviours (compulsions) that he or she feels the urge to repeat over and over. This disorder affects one's quality of life and its symptoms weigh down the individual.

There are several psychopathology and therapy texts available in the market to explain the disorder in detail. But seldom does a person suffering from the disorder try to pen down ways he/she took to overcome the illness. This book is one of a kind where the author (a survivor of the disorder) includes the hitches, trauma, relapse, stumbles and how she survived not just with intervention, but with rigorous self-control, self-introspection,self-forgiveness and self-training.

With the altruistic idea to help fellow individuals suffering with OCD, the author has narrated the path she travelled in three parts – Triggering the change; Dealing with relapse and Recovery. Fatima's inclusion of 'Real life cases' and the Illustrator Fernweh's powerful images in each step of the book will closely guide the reader and make the road to recovery a much smoother one. The author has indeed made every person going through the disorder feel 'You are not alone' and that overcoming OCD is possible.

Kavitha Dhanaraj
Consultant Clinical Psychologist
RCI Reg. No. A08034
Asst. Professor in Psychology
JBAS College for Women, Chennai

DEDICATED TO

My Uncle, 'Chacha'

Your smile is with the stars but the twinkle in

your eyes is forever in my heart

PART 1

Triggering The Change

EVERY DISEASE HAS A CURE SO DOES OCD.

It is not that one is not capable of recovering. It is thus, that one does not know 'how'. Learning to fill in that blank will open doors, the existence of which one wouldn't have dreamt of.

Real life case: People would say, "You will never change." Meanwhile, an inner instinct called out, "It is not that you don't have it in your DNA to be normal. It's just, that your mind had temporarily 'forgotten' how to respond to your environment." The latter drowned out the former. I started observing other 'normal' people and imitating their reactions to stressful situations. This slowly became a habit which grew strong roots in patience and practice. I retrained my brain!

Wheat Stalk

DO YOU GET OVERWHELMED BY THE PROBLEM IN A PROCESS?

Do you react by indulging in an obsessive habit? Realise that the process is only a means to an end. Not an end in itself.

Real life case: I used to obsessively avoid exam preparation by listening to music. I confronted my fears, understood that perfection only belongs to the heavens, and went ahead by reading for a while before putting a pen to the exam paper. That's all it is, a piece of paper. I stopped giving importance to that paper as if it meant 'everything'.

THE 'DOOR' MAY BE CLOSED, BUT YOU HAVE THE KEY.

Pick up the key, unlock the door and enter the building. Repeat process with other buildings. Life suddenly gets simpler.

Real life case: I knew the change must begin from me. So I decided to use the key, that is, the solution which lay within me. Yes, I was afraid. In fact the fear lasted for a long time even after I opened the door to confronting the situation. The more doors I opened, the fear slowly melted away.

SOMETIMES ONE IS REPETITIVE FOR THE SAKE OF AVOIDANCE

A 'mind trick' is thinking, "I regret letting that opportunity slip five years ago. I don't want to feel the same about missing this one five years from now."

Real life case: I realized that repeating an obsessive habit was only a means of 'escapism' from my responsibility. I realized after many precious opportunities slipped by that escapism, or 'obsessive avoidance' is a bottomless pit. So I dived into the heart of my responsibility. I was afraid, but I didn't get hurt. I may have failed, but life went on. That failure was a lesson for the next opportunity to get closer to success.

SOMETIMES AVOIDANCE MAY SEEM UNAVOIDABLE
SIMPLY HIT THE IGNORE BUTTON

A single incident may have a traumatising effect. But one simply walks through it.

Real life case: I was traumatised by severe and unwarranted criticism. It took me some time to realise that such persons are not worth my energy, my emotions, my time or my thoughts. I also discovered another truth: that the person treats many others the same way. I stopped blaming myself for the person's harshness. Note that I say that I did NOT start avoiding the person completely. I simply ignored the person's behaviour, keeping myself busy living my own life.

BE GRACIOUS

Yes, some people are ungracious with us. But we are no better if we choose to react similarly.

Real life case: I was surprised to see how certain people could be gracious with rude persons. It took some time to realise that this is the best way to counter negativity. It was difficult, but I slowly grew a thick skin over a period of time. Don't lose heart when I say 'period of time'. Think of it as a course, where you graduate with honour and grace. Why do I say all this in an anti-OCD book? Because it helps to prevent situations that may cause anxiety and avoid a vicious circle.

ONE PERSON'S ADDICTION IS NOT ONLY ONE'S OWN PROBLEM...

Whatever be the manifestation of OCD, it has the risk of spilling over into other people's lives. This can be via subconscious imitation by others. Take care of yourself, and thereby you are taking care of everyone around you.

Sometimes one may think, "Why should I care about them?" But just think, by ditching the proverbial 'bottle', you are saving the world...A superhero in your own way!

Real life case: I noticed that a child had started washing hands obsessively, just as I had as a toddler. I said, "You are hurting your brain by repeating your behaviour."

I in turn ensured that I followed my own counsel. This 'miracle mix' healed both of us in no time.

Wheat Stalk

LET'S BE WHEAT STALKS

Let's bend, not break. Let us see the gale as only a temporary passerby. Let's not panic.

Real life case: A crisis is a time when we must be flexible. A tree with hard roots finds it difficult to stand upright in a storm. I kept falling down because I expected the problem to solve itself or saw it as irresolvable. I learnt to bend like a wheat stalk in the face of storms, accepting the situation and working through or around it. Sometimes, asking for help from fellow wheat stalks simplified the problem a great deal. I got to keep my 'grains' safe and reaped a full harvest!

Wheat Stalk

THINK THAT THOSE ARE THINGS YOU NEVER NEEDED

It's true. One doesn't 'need' them. It's only a catharsis. Or, it's maybe better suited as a healthy hobby for leisure time.

Real life case: I didn't need to indulge in listening to music as often as earlier. I decided to replace that habit with one of sticking to a routine which directed me to my goals. Indeed, the fear of working towards goals and avoiding them is a reality.

Why do we fear the process of working towards goals?

Fear of failure and the desire for perfection are the two culprits. Well, I learnt that I must simply try my best, let go, and leave the rest to fate. And sometimes, fate turned out to be a pleasant surprise…

YOU ARE CAPABLE

You just need to learn how. Observe. Ask. Emulate. It's just like a toddler learning to walk. Don't be afraid to get up if you fall.

Real life case: I realised that my approach to studying didn't work. So I asked or observed how others studied. I developed a healthy routine, like reading through the day's notes and making points. It's the same with all situations. Don't ever feel incapable. Learn to dance, to drive, to laugh!

INDECISIVENESS IS AN OBSESSION TOO

Follow these steps:

1. Take your time, don't be impulsive.

2. Discuss with people.

3. Realise that the decision is only a means to an end and not an end in itself.

4. Be aware that time is precious. Days lead to months which lead to a whole year! Stress distorts time perception, so quicken your pace

5. Hit the decide button.

6. Respect the decision.

7. Move on.

Real life case: I had a hard time deciding whether or not to continue my studies. Then I felt that it was just a course, one piece of the puzzle that adds up to the rest of my life. The college was just a building made of bricks where learning took place. I decided to go ahead, stuck to my decision, finished the course and went on open doors to a career.

ONE ASKS, "HOW TO PREVENT THIS FROM HAPPENING AGAIN ?"

One can use the memory of an experience and anticipate if it looks like history is doing an encore. That way one can get out before a crisis takes roots. Don't wait for things to worsen. Pull out the weeds from their roots. If they are overwhelmingly widespread, get help. And throw away the weed seeds.

Real life case: I discovered certain signs before having a breakdown. These included becoming reserved, not doing one's daily chores or clearing my work table clutter. I took these as a warning signal and immediately did the healthy opposite. Forcing myself to communicate, sticking to my everyday routine and keeping a neat table kept my mind stress-free. If it was difficult, I would ask for help, sometimes indirectly. I would also get rid of anything that posed a risk of relapse, for instance junk food.

EAT TO LIVE

Clichéd, yes. Irrelevant? No!

Real life case: I decided to get to the root cause of overeating. I discovered it was an attempt to fill the perceived 'emptiness' of life. So I started filling it with mini-adventures: studies, work, hobbies, friends, family and exercise. Sounds easier said than done. However, it turned out to be like a desert safari: slow-paced, humid and exhausting. But it is fun!

WAITING TO CROSS OVER THAT BRIDGE?

Perhaps one is already standing on it.
One was busy looking down instead of
forward. Lift chin and forward march.
Life gets better.

Real life case: I was ready to change
but was waiting for an apparently right
time. It was a case of better now than
later and simply not thinking too much
about embracing change.

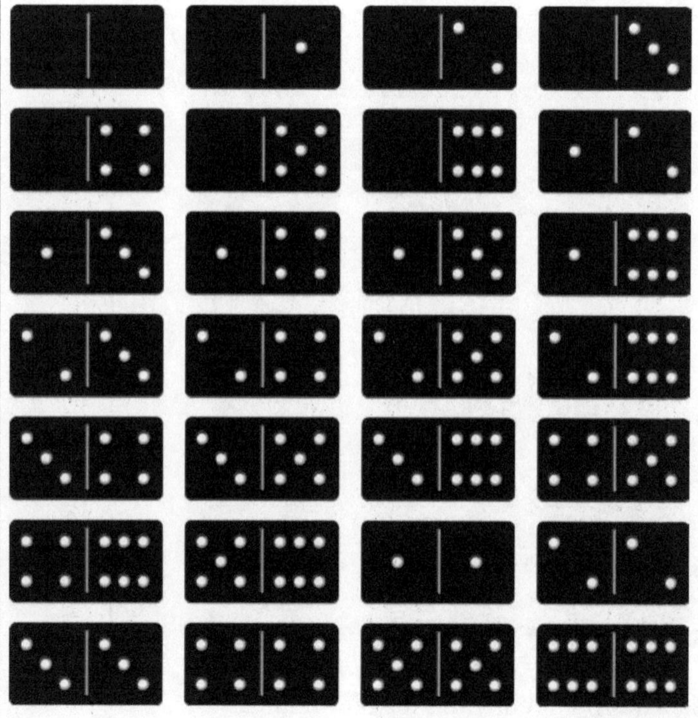

DOES ONE THINK, "THIS IS THE LAST TIME, JUST THIS ONCE...?"

It usually doesn't work. Substitute it with healthier options. Stop stereotyping the path to change. Yes, fruit can be as good as candy. Running can be more satisfying than brooding... get set, go!

Real life case: I can see you nodding your head in agreement when I say how irresistible that piece of cake looked. I stocked up on healthy food within arm's reach for time of cravings. And let last time be the last time.

IT'S NOT ENOUGH TO LET GO OF OLD HABITS

They must be replaced with healthy ones right away or else, old wine reappears in new bottles. If one does relapse, one mustn't lose hope.

Real life case: I didn't start a healthy habit after balancing obsessive reading of storybooks. It led to a new habit-obsessively reading my study material. I was on the verge of a relapse. It was leaving a bitter aftertaste in my life. Realizing the importance of balance, I juggled studying with leisure and time with family and friends. The idea is to not spend too much time on just one activity.

ONE DOESN'T HAVE TO DO EVERYTHING EVERY DAY.

Some things are more enjoyable if touched on a weekly basis. Let's fill the weekdays with priorities.

Real life case: Social media was becoming a menace. It ate into precious hours and led to late nights. I revamped the habit. It was amazing to see how much time I had. I re-discovered my talents, pursued beautiful hobbies and did my homework. Life received a two hundred per cent boost.

WE CAN'T DO EVERYTHING. WE ARE ONLY HUMAN

Don't take on more responsibilities than you can handle. It takes time to reach a level where multitasking becomes easy.

Real life case: I was enthused by my recovery and started taking overdoses of tasks. It was a new kind of OCD which would lead to more anxiety and unrealistic expectations. I received a wonderful piece of advice: "Start simple. Do what interests you. This makes it easier to perform the tasks at hand." For example, even if I was given a specific writing assignment, I would tailor it in such a way that it appealed to me and was easy for me to handle. Lo and behold, a commendable project was born! Meanwhile, I'd read, write or speak on subjects of my interest. Some tasks/courses/careers may not allow this flexibility. Again, prioritise and set realistic goals.

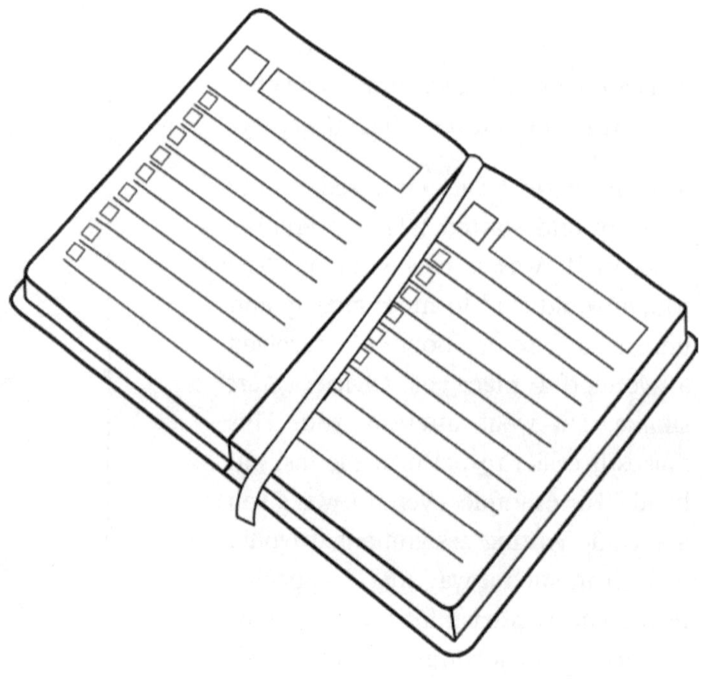

GOALS ARE NOT AN UNREACHABLE PLANET

They are right on earth where we can see them! Point your compass North and start walking.

Real life case: My dreams seemed to be only that, distant dreams. I decided to channelize my interests into action. Letting go of obsessive fear of failure or obsessive desire of perfection was the fuel to my journey forward. I got a planner, listed realistic to-do items and tried my best to stick to them. If they didn't work out, I'd ask, "How can I fix this," and proceed again.

ONE OFTEN SEARCHES FOR ANSWERS EVERYWHERE

The truth often lies within us. Acceptance is a bitter pill to swallow. But the cure is simply too good to deny. It's like shedding off an old skin and transforming into winged bliss. But never let guilt overwhelm you. Forgive yourself, amend the past and move on.

Real life case: I realized that swallowing pride was the first step to being cured. It is not easy to point a finger at oneself. However, it does make miracles...

PART II

Dealing With Relapse

Fatima Yusuf

THIS ISN'T THE END

The sky isn't going to fall.

I will not tremble.

Let them say that the sky falls.

I say it will not crumble;

I will stand tall.

One may fumble

but the sky won't fall.

One learns the ropes

to pulley the stars

and hoist oneself afar.

Yes the baggage is heavy

But I shall lighten my load;

the sky won't fall…

(Adapted from: 'Skyfall', OST,

Skyfall)

Fatima Yusuf

LOOK UP SEE THE SILVER LINING ?

Now instead of waiting, let us build the stairway with our bare hands. Yes, the cloud seems menacing. But it is harmless. It is the crucial rain-bearer of one's hard work before one enjoys the crops.

Real life case: Hope beckoned after a relapse. But the fear of confronting similar situations again was profound. I channelled this 'cloud' of fear into a positive energy and used it a driving force. It helped to face life and reap rewards.

WAITING FOR THE LIGHT AT THE END OF THE TUNNEL?

Notice the torch in your hand? Switch it on. Be the light. Let your effort be the battery. Shine on.

Real life case: Sometimes hope seemed invisible. I decided to spray paint it with my own effort to make it more apparent. Like after a relapse. After stumbling a bit in the dark, I managed to find the light switch and... walah! Dawn was here.

LET GO

Just. Let. Go. Don't worry. One will not fall. One will learn to walk without the cane.

Real life case: I understood that letting go of reading too much fiction had to be a quick split rather than a messy long drawn process. It seemed strange at first. In fact after a relapse, I found I wasn't interested in reading anymore. I took time to slowly gain the leaning towards reading again, but only those books which added value to my language skills, values or interests. It was no longer a desperate attempt for grabbing a support system. It became one of the many windows of the building which is my life, opening only when I chose.

THEY SAY WHEN IN ROME DO AS ROMANS DO…

However, another saying goes: be careful of whom you spend time with, for you may become like them. It may become your Atlantis. But sometimes, one can't help living in Rome. If not possible to evade, keep busy manoeuvring. Remember what happened the last time when did/ didn't do something, while citing a lame excuse.

Real life case: It is difficult to react differently to a situation than how a close acquaintance would. I would repeat this behaviour, namely of panicking in a crisis, and not get any positive results. So I trained myself to be different, to be calm and to think clearly.

Wheat Stalk

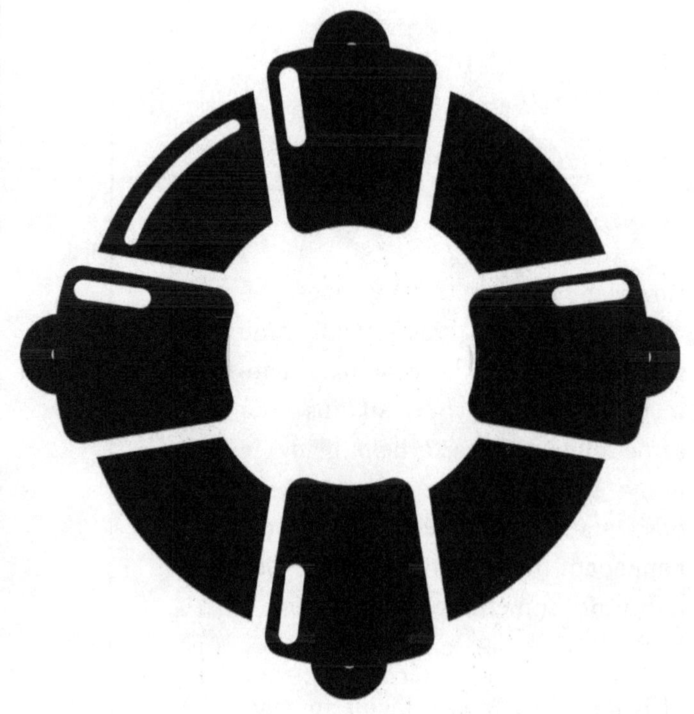

SOMETIMES A LIFEBUOY HELPS

But let's not be clingy with the lifebuoy.
Its duty is to give hope. Ours is to take
encouragement and keep swimming.

Real life case: Yes, asking for help is
sometimes necessary. But I became
too dependent on the helper. I realized
it was another obsession, so it was
replaced with a mixture of moderation
and self-help.

IT IS NOT ENOUGH TO SAVE WHEN PLAYING SHOPPING CUSTOMER

Maintenance of products can turn out to be a costly task. One must sometimes ask, "Is it necessary?", "Is it too old?", "Is it an object of obsession, not mere sentiment?" and, "Is the upkeep worth it?" Let go. Let the new season bring a refreshing change. More space, less clutter, more savings.

Real life case: I stopped overspending. Yet, I did not get rid of old things. Maintaining them was expensive. A balance was necessary. Hoarding was replaced with de-cluttered space.

FINDING COMPLACENCY TOO CLOSE FOR COMFORT ?

Don't wait for a disaster to strike. Nip it in the bud. Yes, chemical imbalance is a pain. Fight it. Fight for normalcy. Fight for dignity. Fight with grace and honour by your side.

Real life case: I would sometimes escape into an unhealthy carefree attitude. This would lead to procrastination. It was not easy, but I conquered it with self-respect, prioritising and implementing. I was greeted with respect and recognition. Above all, I found normalcy. Rather, it came looking for me.

SPARKS MAY APPEAR AFTER RECOVERY

They are nothing but traces of benign DNA. What is important is that they don't ignite.

Real life case: Sometimes I would get the urge to start listening to music for hours again. I may begin, but would stop myself with one tune. I made sure that the spark didn't catch fire.

IF THE SPARK DOES IGNITE DON'T PANIC

It can be put out. Don't panic. Use your memory to live the same routine life and eventually the air will be clear again.

Real life case: I had a relapse. I dusted off the ashes, started the same normal routine and slowly, the smoke of the past disappeared. But the memory of the incident was a reminder to be more careful in future.

YES, SOMETIMES THE SPARKS COME ALTOGETHER

Challenge them with your own fireworks. The fact that you are reading this shows you have achieved the goal of self-awareness. Yes there were bloopers. But the sun didn't stop mid-orbit. Neither should you.

Real life case: It is not easy when facing a relapse. I fought back, knowing that having achieved self-awareness earlier was a plus point. Recovery was faster. Everything in nature moves on. A field takes roots again after a devastating storm, because the farmer simply came out of the shelter and went on with his or her daily routine.

IMPULSE CONTROL IS A MIGHTY HORSE TO TAME

Sometimes there is no other way than asking for help.

Real life case: Before a potential relapse, I would sometimes undergo insurmountable emotions. Talking to friends, family or a therapist saved me.

Fatima Yusuf

ONE SHOULD WAIT FOR THE MOMENT TO PASS

Don't let it overwhelm you. Don't lose your grip. Wait awhile and let the mist clear. Then tread carefully.

Real life case: I would ignore the urge to restart an obsessive habit. After some time, everything would fall into place.

SOMETIMES THE PASSING MOMENT LASTS LONGER THAN EXPECTED

But when it clears, there is surprise that it even happened. There is no easy explanation. But there is relief that is passed. Look for warning signals next time and take action.

Real life case: I would sometimes struggle for a long time before the urge went away. I didn't try to analyze it. That would simply add to my worries. Just taking action when warning signs appear is enough.

LITTLE DROPS OF LAVA MAKE A VOLCANO

Don't let things build up to a point where they become overwhelming. Be it sadness or anger, errands or duties, priorities or projects.

Real life case: I used to let assignments pile up till the last minute. Panic mode was inevitable. I realized the reason was not only mere procrastination, but a fear of failure. I wanted everything to be perfect, so would 'wait' for the best resources or ideas to accumulate. I did this instead of being proactive. End result: deadlines missed or sloppy work. To set things right, I started performing the task RIGHT NOW. If there was more than one, I would write a list to keep track of priorities. Then I would work on them one by one, one after another. End result: I would check off agenda points, meet deadlines and avoid anxiety. Sounds simple to a non-OCDian. But believe me; it can take some practice when OCD has prevailed earlier. Don't let this last point be an excuse to procrastinate ;)

OPPORTUNITY IS OFTEN DISGUISED

Learn to see a chance to move further in every fall. It's like stumbling when learning to ride a bicycle.

Real life case: I took EVERY letdown as a lesson. It was difficult to see a silver lining in every dark cloud. But I now know that overcoming OCD is a constant learning process. However, it is simply exhilarating to achieve even small milestones.

LIFE TEACHES LESSONS ONE PAGE AT A TIME

Sometimes revision is necessary. Read carefully, don't rush.

Real life case: In order to avoid relapse, I would come back to the lessons learnt which I am sharing with you. Revising would boost my life exam's grade sheet.

JUST KEEP SWIMMING

Tomorrow? Today? Tonight? No.

The change starts now.

Real life case: I didn't want to drown in OCD. I kept swimming even when it was cold and dark, and the water was deep. And I have reached the shore safely.

CHANGE IS NOT AN OPTION

Remember, one has to step forward, not wait cooped up inside the comfort zone. Yes it's frightening, but take the plunge and find yourself flying high.

Real life case: After recognizing that I could change my life after a relapse, I stepped into the territory of normalcy. The trek along the land became simple when it was obvious that it's just a matter of perspective whether I was climbing a mountain. When I ignored fear, the mountain became smaller. And I chose to walk up that hill. I chose to leave the valley of darkness behind, which I had gotten so used to. It's like switching on the light after a period of time. One narrows one's eyes because of the brightness, but that 'fear' is just a reaction to the unknown. I became acclimatized to the light and now take in the sights gladly.

EVOLUTION THEORY IS REAL... IN OCD!

One evolves as a person when dealing with relapse. Take it as a new chapter in life.

Real life case: I was the author of my own story. I saw that some actions didn't make sense. So I would write a new page, with the ink of self-introspection and self-forgiveness. A book of new beginnings would be my prize.

Fatima Yusuf

BEING STEREOTYPED CAN BE A GOOD THING

It serves as a reminder of what kind of change is necessary. Besides being a good chance to prove them wrong!

Real life case: There is a good thing in constructive criticism. I took it as a free lesson to change. I swallowed pride and surprised the critic with the new me.

PART III

Recovery

I WILL SURVIVE

At first I was afraid

I was petrified

Kept thinking I could never live with
the past by my side

But then I spent so many nights

Thinking how I did me wrong

And I grew strong

And I learnt how to get along

And so I'm back

From my hiding place

I just walked in with a smile upon my
face

I should have opened the lock long
ago

I should have used those keys

If I'd known for just a second I'd be a
better brand new me

Go on now go!

I'm walking out the door

I'm not turning around now

I'm ready for more

Wasn't I the one who dragged and hurt
me with a lie

I thought I'd crumble

I thought I'd lay down and die

Oh no not I

I will survive

As long as I know how to love myself

I know I'll stay alive

I've got all my life to live

I've got all my love to give

I will survive

I will survive!

(Adapted from Gloria Gaynor's 'I will survive')

BE YOUR OWN DIAMOND POLISHER

Sometimes when you want something done, you have to do it yourself, as the cliché goes. Take up the mantle of responsibility and dazzle away.

Real life case: I admit it, I studied very hard for my exams. It was not easy. But like a child learning to ride a bicycle, I stumbled and slowly became an expert. This attitude applies to any scenario in life.

THE STORM HAS PASSED.
YOU ARE STILL STANDING.

Congratulations. Recovery is real.

Real life case: I experienced a test of my recovery during a significant crisis. It was exhilarating to discover my inner strength!

IT TAKES 365 DAYS FOR THE EARTH TO REVOLVE AROUND THE SUN

Everything takes its natural course of time, with our effort of course. But it finally happens. Months, even years may pass. But one fine day you wake up. Your eyes open. It's better late than never.

Real life case: I knew, it would take time for me to fully recover. However like set time periods in nature, I passed the goalpost one inch at a time. I may not have been a prize winner in that scenario, but I had crossed the finish line. That's what matters the most.

CHANGE ISN'T LIKE AUTOMATIC GEARS

It is about replacing the old habit(s) with a new habit(s) and performing it every day. It will take time. Be patient. But don't slow down.

Real life case: My biggest lesson after recovering from relapse was that I couldn't expect normalcy to maintain itself. I learnt to manually shift the gears of life and steer amidst the traffic of everyday issues.

LIFE ISN'T INSTANT COFFEE

It's a big pot of masala tea to be brewed, one ingredient at a time. Weeks, months, maybe even years will pass before the desired flavour is achieved. But the wait is worth it. Until then, enjoy each day as a tasting ceremony. But don't be complacent, keep stirring.

Real life case: Normalcy didn't arrive one fine day. I invited it in, welcomed it with practice and of course, the brew of patience.

ONE MUST MAKE AMENDS.

One must, without doubt, make amends.

Real life case: I wanted to make up for the past. Writing this book was one way. I also became more forgiving of others. Nobody is perfect.

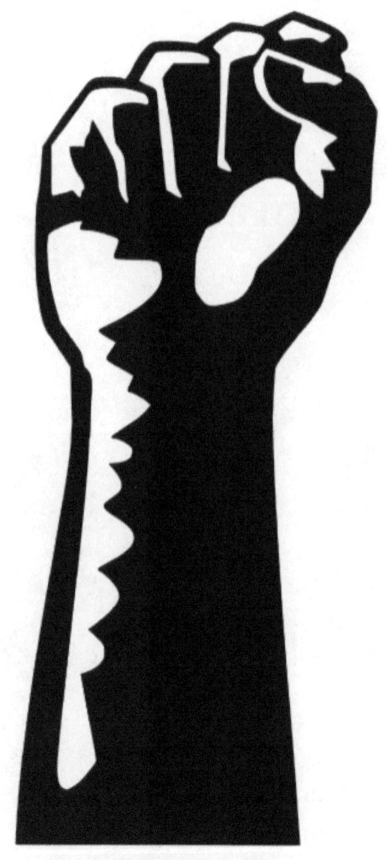

RECOVERY: DOES IT FLOAT ABOVE OR FLEE AWAY?

Beneath normalcy may lie small but strong remnants of the past. The red lines warn that relapse is possible. But there is that which one calls 'beneficial stubbornness'- that one will continue to be normal.

Real life case: Sometimes, I felt the craving to read obsessively again. I put my foot down, became strict with myself and frightened the urge away. I had enough faith in myself to know that I had changed.

ONE IS SOMETIMES GLAD ABOUT THIS PROBLEM.

It means, those dear to us have been spared of the same. This should not happen even to an enemy.

Real life case: I am happy that I could learn a lesson from my recovery and pass it onto others. However I am also glad that my near and dear ones were spared. It is not easy to be selfless in an OCD situation, but it does make life more beautiful.

IT'S NOT ENOUGH TO START THE NEW YEAR WELL.

Perseverance is the lofty ladder of life.

Real life case: I was having a great start after recovery. However, it was a challenge to maintain normal habits until they became ingrained. I climbed the ladder and never looked back. The year ended well.

ONE MUST PRACTICE WHAT ONE PREACHES.

One must keep living the dream. One must retrain oneself to run. One must keep trying until practice becomes a personal trait.

Real life case: It is easy to give advice. One must follow it too. I started writing this book before I fully recovered. It was mostly a message to the self to keep practicing normal behaviour. More than 'preaching', I believe in sharing. You can too :)

SOMETIMES ONE FORGETS THE PAST

It's good to move on. But take time to remember your battles. You made it here because of that journey. Keep the faith. Be kind to yourself. Give yourself a pat on the back.

Real life case: I would feel dismayed at a 'situation' but then recollect I had survived worse. Silently praising myself, I would face it head on.

SING TO THE NEW YOU.

Croon to that person, you can't be hurt
by what happened in the past.

Real life case: Some memories haunted
me. However if seemed to reach out, I
swatted them away like flies, knowing
they were just a harmless piece of data
about the past recoded in my mind.

WOW. SO THIS IS WHAT NORMAL FEELS LIKE

One knows what is black, white and grey. The grey cannot be erased. But it's okay. One can just feel like… living normally.

Real life case: I knew that there is no such thing as flawlessness. Even the beauty of hand-made pottery comes from imperfection. I accepted myself with my past whole-heartedly.

PETALS MAY BLOOM THEN WILT

There are always new flowers that follow. Winter is the predecessor of spring.

Real life case: I let go of things. I accepted death of near and dear ones. I accepted new events. But there was always a fresh bouquet of flowers waiting to be plucked.

JUST FLY.

Soaring seagulls don't have the time to squawk.

Real life case: Talking about change is easy. However I started practicing normalcy during writing this book. And realised that the less said, the better. After all, we both have a long way to fly before reaching the sky.

THERE ARE BAD DAYS.

But they pass you by. You will survive. You will make today the base for a good tomorrow.

Real life case: We are only human. What made me more humane was forgiving oneself, learning from one's past and using it as foundation for tomorrow.

SHIFT

DELETE

PHANTOM OCD: HIT DELETE

There are times when stray OCD impulsive thoughts occur even after recovery. Don't think about them. Simply hit the delete button and create new files of normalcy.

Real life case: Just as some amputees feel 'phantom' pain in their missing limbs, I would get thoughts that may seem to hark of the past. But I just clicked Shift + Delete, not even giving room in the Recycle bin of my mind. How? I wouldn't even think of it, just as I wouldn't one think one second about a stray speck of dust floating aimlessly in the vast universe.

RECOVERY CAN THROW SOME SURPRISES

One can't do what one used to obsess about.

Real life case: The very act is repelling: Reading fiction for more than thirty minutes, or watching television for more than an hour or a half. But at least now one has more time to follow suppressed passions and hobbies. What a sweet surprise!

YES. VERY FEW UNDERSTAND

Demand equality. Work hard. Yes, it's very hard but you must change. There is no guarantee that people with prejudice will accept you but at least you would have changed. There is no greater reward than that.

Real life case: I didn't expect everyone to understand me. Instead, I trotted down my own path in life, happy if it converged with others' or even if was a solitary walk.

TRYING TO GET USED TO THE NEW YOU? DOES THE MIRROR SHOW AN ACCOMPLISHED STRANGER?

Accept the recovery proudly. Don't just stand in front of the mirror. Run to your new life.

Real life case: Sometimes, I would feel too strange for comfort in my new avatar but I realised it was senseless to question my recovery. One doesn't keep thinking about a physical illness after being cured. So why in OCD?

POLITE CONVERSATION

If they say, "You are done."

Just smile and reply, "I've just begun."

If they jeer, "You have fallen."

Get up and say, "I have risen."

If they shout, "You have erred."

Tell them with chin up, "I have learned."

If they look down on you,

Lift your head up to the sky so blue.

For they will find

That for you,

The finish line has been left far behind...

IT'S NOT ABOUT THEM.

Life isn't about proving yourself to others.

Real life case: I must admit, popular entertainment is very influential. If you look closely, even in cartoons, there is a lot of focus on 'reactions' and 'responses', which leads to impulsive actions by the protagonist. I trained myself to get out of this subconscious influence. Again, note that we cannot blame our environment for everything. We all have the power to make decisions. With that power, comes responsibility.

SET SAIL TODAY.

Bon voyage. Have a safe and OCD-free
journey.

www.ingramcontent.com/pod-product-compliance
Lightning Source LLC
Chambersburg PA
CBHW051451130726
47987CB00005B/2264